Give thanks for big and small,
short and tall, everyone, over all
give thanks from your heart.
–Unknown

Pumpkin Coffeecake

2 16-oz. pkgs. pound
   cake mix
4 t. pumpkin pie spice
2 t. baking soda
3/4 c. water
15-oz. can pumpkin

4 eggs
3/4 c. brown sugar, packed
3/4 c. chopped walnuts
1/2 c. all-purpose flour
1/3 c. butter

Combine cake mix, pumpkin pie spice and baking soda. Blend in water, pumpkin and eggs; beat until well mixed. Pour half the batter into a greased 13"x9" baking pan. In a separate bowl, blend together brown sugar, walnuts and flour; cut in butter until crumbly. Sprinkle half of crumb mixture on top of batter. Pour remaining batter into pan and sprinkle remaining crumb mixture on top. Bake at 325 degrees for 50 minutes. Serves 6 to 8.

Tuck family photos into florist card holders and arrange with colorful mums...what a terrific Autumn centerpiece!

Cinnamon Rolls

3/4 c. warm water
2 pkgs. active dry yeast
1/2 c. sugar
1 t. salt
2 eggs

1/2 c. shortening
1/2 c. plus 2 T. butter,
   divided
4 c. all-purpose flour
cinnamon-sugar to taste

Stir together water, yeast, sugar, salt, eggs, shortening, 1/2 cup butter and flour; knead about 5 minutes on a lightly floured board. Let dough rise in a lightly oiled bowl until double in bulk. Roll into a large rectangle until dough is 1/4-inch thick. Spread with remaining butter and sprinkle with cinnamon-sugar. Roll up jelly roll-style and cut into one-inch slices. Place slices on a greased baking sheet and bake at 350 degrees for 15 to 20 minutes or until golden. Makes 12 to 14 servings.

Looking for a simple placecard idea? Write names on cards, punch a hole in the corner of each and slip over the stems of apples or mini pumpkins!

Spiced Apple Tea

4 cinnamon-flavored teabags
3 c. boiling water
5 T. honey

3 c. unsweetened apple juice
Garnish: apple slices and
 cinnamon sticks

Brew tea in boiling water. Remove tea bags; add honey and apple juice. Simmer until heated through. Pour tea into mugs; garnish each with an apple slice and cinnamon stick. Serves 4.

Orange-Apple Cider

1 gal. apple cider
3 cinnamon sticks
peel of one orange

1/4 t. nutmeg
Garnish: orange slices and
 cinnamon sticks

Place all ingredients in a slow cooker; heat, covered, on high for one hour. Reduce heat to low and keep warm until ready to serve; remove orange peel before serving. Garnish each serving with an orange slice and cinnamon stick. Makes about 16 cups.

Take lots of pictures
of the family this
Thanksgiving. Placed in
a scrapbook along with
best-loved recipes, it'll
be a terrific
collection of memories.

Glazed Spiced Pecans

3/4 c. sugar
1 egg white
2-1/2 t. water
1/2 t. cinnamon
1/4 t. allspice

1/4 t. ground cloves
1/4 t. nutmeg
1/2 t. salt
8 c. pecans

Combine all ingredients in a large bowl; spread onto a lightly greased baking sheet. Bake at 225 degrees for 30 minutes. Cool on wax paper. Makes 8 cups.

Pumpkin Dip

4 c. powdered sugar, sifted
2 8-oz. pkgs. cream
   cheese, softened

15-oz. can pumpkin
2 t. cinnamon
1 t. ground ginger

In a large bowl, combine sugar and cream cheese; beat until well blended. Blend in remaining ingredients. Refrigerate until ready to serve. Serve with sliced apples and vanilla wafers. Serves 8 to 10.

Cheesy Cauliflower

1-1/4 t. mayonnaise
1-1/4 t. mustard
1 head cauliflower, chopped
    and cooked

1/4 c. butter, sliced
3/4 c. grated Parmesan
    cheese

In a small mixing bowl, combine mayonnaise and mustard.
Place cauliflower in an ungreased 2-quart baking dish; spread
with mustard mixture and dot with butter. Sprinkle with
cheese. Bake at 375 degrees for 30 minutes. Makes 4 to
6 servings.

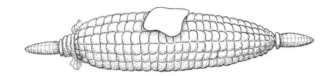

Baked Creamed Corn

2 eggs, beaten
1 c. milk
1 T. sugar
1 t. salt
2 T. butter

1/8 t. pepper
1 c. creamed corn
1/4 c. shredded Cheddar
    cheese

In a large mixing bowl, combine eggs, milk, sugar, salt, butter,
pepper and corn; mix well. Pour into a greased 2-quart baking
dish. Sprinkle cheese over top. Bake at 350 degrees for
30 minutes. Makes 3 to 4 servings.

*An oh-so-simple harvest greeting! Tie ears of Indian
corn to a length of jute and hang across the front door.*

Yam & Apple Bake

6 to 8 yams
6 to 8 apples, cored, peeled
   and sliced
1 c. sugar

1/4 c. cornstarch
1 t. salt
2 c. boiling water
1/2 c. butter

Boil yams 3 to 4 minutes; peel and cube. Layer yams and apples in a buttered 13"x9" baking dish; set aside. Combine sugar, cornstarch and salt in a saucepan. Add boiling water and butter; stir over medium heat until mixture comes to a boil. Pour sauce over yams and apples. Bake at 350 degrees for one hour. Serves 8 to 10.

Decorate a welcome wreath for the garden gate
with giant sunflower heads and bittersweet!

Vanilla-Glazed Sweet Potatoes

3 lbs. sweet potatoes, peeled
1/4 c. butter
1/4 c. brown sugar, packed
1 t. salt
1 t. orange zest
1/4 t. pepper
3 T. orange juice
1 T. vanilla extract
1/2 c. chopped pecans

Boil sweet potatoes in water until tender; drain. Cool slightly, then cut into 1/4-inch slices. Arrange slices in a greased 13"x9" baking dish, overlapping slightly. In a small saucepan, melt butter over low heat. Add brown sugar, salt, orange zest, pepper, orange juice and vanilla, stirring until combined. Heat, but do not allow to boil; remove from heat and brush sauce evenly over potato slices. Broil 6 inches from heat until golden, about 6 to 7 minutes. Sprinkle with pecans. Serves 6.

Hollowed-out artichokes make beautiful votives! Slip them inside terra cotta pots and line up on the mantel, porch steps or on a buffet table.

Garlic Mashed Potatoes

2 to 4 cloves garlic	2 t. salt
2 T. plus 1 t. butter, divided	1/4 c. sour cream
1 t. olive oil	1/2 c. warm milk
5 potatoes, peeled and chopped	1/4 c. fresh chives, chopped
	salt and pepper to taste

To roast garlic, peel each clove and place in a one-pint oven-proof baker. Add one teaspoon butter and olive oil. Bake, covered, at 325 degrees for 45 minutes. The cloves should be golden, but not brown. Remove from oven, cool slightly, then mash with a fork; set aside. Place potatoes in a 4-1/2 quart saucepan; add enough water to completely cover potatoes. Stir in salt and bring to a boil. Reduce heat to a simmer and continue to cook until tender, about 15 to 20 minutes. Drain; mash with an electric mixer. Add remaining butter and continue to mash until well blended. Add sour cream, milk, chives, garlic, salt and pepper. Makes 8 servings.

Freeze leftover mashed potatoes in individual muffin cups. When frozen, toss in freezer bags and just microwave when needed...what a time saver!

Roast Turkey & Gravy

8 slices bacon, crisply
   cooked and crumbled
1 c. butter, softened
3 T. fresh sage, chopped
salt and pepper to taste
16-lb. turkey
3 c. leeks, white and green
   parts, chopped

8 fresh sage sprigs
3 bay leaves, crumbled
4-1/2 c. chicken broth;
   divided
Garnish: fresh sage and
   parsley

Combine bacon, butter and chopped sage in a medium bowl. Season with salt and pepper; set aside. Pat turkey dry with paper towels and season cavity with salt and pepper. Place leeks, sage sprigs and bay leaves in cavity. Loosen skin on turkey breast and spread 1/3 cup butter mixture over meat, under skin. Place turkey on rack set in large roasting pan and rub 2 tablespoons butter mixture over outside of turkey. Set aside 1/3 cup butter mix for gravy; reserve remaining for basting. Position rack in bottom third of oven. Pour 1/3 cup broth over turkey and roast turkey at 350 degrees until thermometer inserted into thickest part of inner thigh registers 180 degrees. Every 30 minutes baste turkey with 1/3 cup broth; brush with butter mixture once each basting. Continue for 3 hours. Transfer turkey to a platter and let stand 30 minutes. To prepare gravy, pour pan juices into large glass measuring cup; spoon off fat and discard. Pour juices into a saucepan, add 2 cups broth and bring to a boil. Continue to boil until liquid is reduced to 2 cups. Whisk in reserved butter mixture; season to taste. Serves 16 to 20.

Make it a Thanksgiving to remember always...gather
family & friends, share food, laughter,
memories and traditions.

Apple Cider Turkey

5 to 7-lb. turkey breast
1 c. apple cider vinegar
1/4 c. salt
1/4 c. pepper
1/4 c. oil
2 T. dried parsley

Place turkey breast in a large oven roasting bag. Combine apple cider vinegar, salt, pepper, oil and parsley in a container with a tight-fitting lid; secure lid and shake until mixed thoroughly. Pour over turkey and bake at 300 degrees for 2-1/2 to 3-1/2 hours or until a meat thermometer registers 180 degrees. Serves 6 to 8.

Herbed Rice Pilaf

1/4 c. butter
2 c. instant long-grain rice,
    uncooked
1 c. celery, chopped
1/2 c. onion, chopped
4 c. chicken broth
1 t. Worcestershire sauce
1 t. soy sauce
1 t. dried oregano
1 t. dried thyme

Melt butter in a saucepan; stir in rice, celery and onion. Sauté until rice is lightly browned and celery and onion become tender. Transfer to a lightly oiled 2-quart casserole dish. Whisk together remaining ingredients and pour over rice. Cover and bake at 325 degrees for 50 minutes or until rice is tender. Makes 8 servings.

Don't save them for "someday," make sweet memories now...use Grandma's china and good silver!

Make-Ahead Dinner Rolls

1 pkg. active dry yeast
1/2 c. sugar
1 c. warm milk
2 eggs, beaten

1/2 c. butter, melted
1 t. salt
4 c. all-purpose flour

Combine first 3 ingredients in a mixing bowl and let stand for
30 minutes. Add eggs, butter and salt. Blend in flour, 2 cups at
a time. Let dough stand at room temperature overnight. The
next morning, divide dough in half, rolling each into a 9-inch
circle. Cut each circle into 12 equal wedges; roll each up
beginning at wide end. Place on a well-greased baking sheet;
let stand until ready to bake. Rolls can stand for 8 to 12 hours,
but for best results, don't exceed 6 hours. Bake at 375 degrees
for 12 to 15 minutes. Makes 2 dozen.

Take a home video while everyone shares something
they're thankful for...great to watch in years to come!

Triple Cranberry Sauce

1 c. frozen cranberry juice
    concentrate, thawed
1/3 c. sugar
12 oz. cranberries, rinsed
    and drained

1/2 c. dried cranberries
3 T. orange marmalade
2 T. orange juice
2 t. orange zest
1/4 t. allspice

Combine first 4 ingredients in a saucepan. Bring mixture to a boil, stirring often until dried berries begin to soften and fresh berries pop, about 7 minutes. Remove from heat; stir in remaining ingredients. Cool completely; cover and chill 2 hours. Makes 2-1/2 cups.

Cranberry Relish

1 red apple, cored and
    halved
2 seedless oranges, halved
12 oz. cranberries, rinsed
    and drained

1 c. sugar
3-oz. pkg. cranberry
    gelatin mix
1/2 c. chopped walnuts

Process fruit in a food processor. Add remaining ingredients and mix again. Chill before serving. Makes 8 to 10 servings.

Hold hands around the Thanksgiving table...a
sweet way to begin the celebration.

Homestyle Stuffing

1 carrot, finely diced
1 onion, finely diced
2 stalks celery, finely diced
1/4 c. butter
1 loaf white bread, torn
10-3/4 oz. can cream of
    mushroom soup

10-3/4 oz. can cream of
    chicken soup
water
salt and pepper to taste

Combine carrot, onion, celery and butter in a saucepan. Sauté over medium heat until vegetables are tender; toss in bread and set aside. Blend soups and one soup can of water together; add one cup soup mixture to bread mixture and set aside remaining soup mixture. Salt and pepper bread to taste; stir well. Shape stuffing into 3-inch balls and place in a lightly greased 13"x9" baking dish. Pour remaining soup mixture over top; cover and bake at 350 degrees for 30 to 40 minutes or until heated through. Makes 12 servings.

Begin a new tradition...use a special tablecloth and ask everyone to sign it with fabric markers. Bring it out year after year.

Green Beans Supreme

1 onion, sliced
1 T. fresh parsley, snipped
3 T. butter, divided
2 T. all-purpose flour
1/2 t. lemon zest
1/2 t. salt
1/8 t. pepper
1/2 c. milk

1 c. sour cream
2 9-oz. pkgs. frozen
   French-style green
   beans, cooked
1/2 c. shredded Cheddar
   cheese
1/4 c. bread crumbs

Cook onion and parsley in 2 tablespoons butter until onion is tender. Whisk in flour, lemon zest, salt and pepper. Stir in milk; heat until thick and bubbly. Add sour cream and beans; heat through. Spoon into an ungreased 2-quart baking dish; sprinkle with cheese. Melt remaining butter and toss with bread crumbs; sprinkle on top of beans. Broil 3 to 4 inches from heat source until golden. Makes 4 to 6 servings.

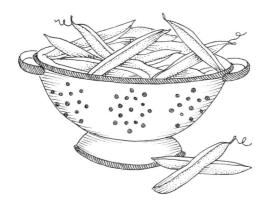

Football on the lawn, parades on T.V. or puzzles on the coffee table...spend time with those you love most.

Heavenly Potatoes

1 onion, finely chopped
2 T. butter
24-oz. pkg. frozen shredded
    hashbrowns, thawed
2 c. sharp Cheddar cheese,
    grated

10-3/4 oz. can cream of
    chicken soup
2 c. sour cream
salt and pepper to taste

Sauté onion in butter until tender; combine with remaining ingredients. Pour into a lightly greased 2-quart baking dish; bake at 350 degrees for one hour. Makes 8 to 10 servings.

Cheddar Biscuits with Garlic Butter

2 c. biscuit baking mix
2/3 c. milk
1/2 c. shredded Cheddar
    cheese

1/4 c. butter, melted
1/2 t. garlic powder

Stir together baking mix, milk and cheese until soft dough forms. Beat vigorously for 30 seconds. Drop by heaping tablespoonfuls onto a lightly greased baking sheet. Bake at 400 degrees for 8 to 10 minutes or until golden. In a small bowl, combine butter and garlic powder; brush over warm biscuits while still on baking sheet. Makes 10 to 12 biscuits.

Make Thanksgiving a snap and hold a progressive dinner.
Each family prepares one part of the meal, then visits
each home to enjoy it...a great way to catch up
and no one person does all the cooking!

Country Glazed Ham

10 to 12-lb. fully cooked   1/4 c. water
    smoked ham, skin
    removed and fat trimmed

Place ham in a shallow roasting pan and add water. Bake at
325 degrees, approximately 16 minutes per pound. If ham
browns too quickly, place a tent of foil over it. Do not seal.
When done, remove from oven and allow to rest while making
the glaze; spread glaze over ham. Serves 16 to 20.

Glaze:

peels of 6 oranges,   1/3 c. currant jelly
    thinly sliced   3/4 c. orange marmalade
2 c. water   4 T. beef broth

Combine orange peels and water in saucepan and boil for
10 minutes; drain and repeat. Combine jelly, marmalade and
orange peels in saucepan and simmer for 10 minutes. Remove
from heat and stir in broth.

Creamy Butternut Soup

5 lbs. butternut squash,
    peeled and chopped
1-1/2 lbs. apples, peeled,
    cored and quartered
1-inch cinnamon stick

2 qts. chicken broth
1-1/2 c. butter
1/3 c. maple syrup
1/2 t. nutmeg
1 pt. light cream

Steam squash, apples and cinnamon stick together until
squash is tender. Remove cinnamon stick; place remaining
mixture through a food mill and place in a large stockpot. Stir
in chicken broth, butter, syrup and nutmeg; simmer
15 minutes. In a small saucepan, heat cream until hot, but not
boiling. Add to soup mixture and stir well. Serves 8.

Pumpkin Farmer's Casserole

15-oz. can pumpkin
12-oz. can evaporated milk
1/4 c. butter, melted
1/2 c. sugar

4 eggs
2 t. cinnamon
1/4 t. nutmeg
1/4 t. ground cloves

Mix all ingredients together in a large mixing bowl. Pour into a
lightly greased 2-quart baking dish. Bake at 325 degrees for
45 minutes or until set. Makes 8 servings.

Create a cornucopia of fruit, nuts, colorful leaves and
dried herbs in a big wooden bowl...a quick & easy
Autumn centerpiece.

Banana & Walnut Bread

1/4 c. shortening
1/4 c. margarine
1 c. sugar
2 eggs
1 c. bananas, mashed
1-1/2 c. all-purpose flour
1 t. baking soda

1/4 t. salt
1/4 t. cinnamon
1/2 c. quick-cooking oats,
   uncooked
1/2 c. blueberries
1/2 c. chopped walnuts

In a large bowl, cream shortening, margarine and sugar together. Add eggs, one at a time, mixing well after each addition; stir in bananas. In a separate bowl, sift together flour, baking soda, salt and cinnamon; fold in oats, blueberries and walnuts. Carefully blend dry mixture into the creamed mixture, stirring only to moisten. Pour batter into a well-greased 9"x5" loaf pan. Bake at 350 degrees for 50 to 55 minutes, or until toothpick inserted into center comes out clean. Cool for 10 minutes before removing from pan. Allow bread to cool completely on a wire rack. Serves 6 to 8.

Toss lots of plump pillows on the sofa for
those after-dinner naps!

Classics

Perfectly Pecan Pie

9-inch refrigerated pie crust
2 T. butter
1/2 c. sugar
2 eggs, beaten
2 T. all-purpose flour

1/4 t. salt
1 t. vanilla extract
1 c. corn syrup
1-1/2 c. chopped pecans

Line a pan with pie crust; set aside. Cream butter and sugar together; add eggs, flour, salt, vanilla and corn syrup, mixing well. Fold in pecans; pour into pie crust. Bake at 350 degrees for 45 to 50 minutes or until set. Cool and serve slightly warm. Makes 8 servings.

Maple Indian Pudding

1 c. cornmeal
1 qt. whole milk
1/2 c. brown sugar

1 c. whipping cream
1/2 c. pure maple syrup
1/8 t. nutmeg

Whisk cornmeal into milk in a heavy saucepan over high heat; stir until slightly thickened, about 5 minutes. Remove from heat and stir in brown sugar; add whipping cream, syrup and nutmeg. Pour pudding in a buttered 1-1/2 quart baking dish. Bake at 275 degrees for 4 hours until pudding is bubbly and top is golden. Allow to rest 30 minutes before serving. Serves 4 to 6.

Make pie crust ahead of time...roll it out, fit it inside the pie plate, cover with wax paper and slip inside a freezer bag. One less thing to do on the big day!

Harvest Apple Cheesecake

2 c. graham cracker crumbs
1/3 c. brown sugar, packed
1/2 c. butter, melted
    and divided
1 T. cinnamon
3 apples, cored, peeled and
    sliced into 12 rings
4 eggs

3/4 c. sugar
8-oz. container ricotta
    cheese
8-oz. pkg. cream cheese,
    softened
2 t. vanilla extract
8 oz. whipping cream
Garnish: cinnamon

Combine crumbs, brown sugar, 1/4 cup butter and cinnamon.
Press on bottom and part way up sides of a 9" springform pan.
In a skillet, sauté apple rings on both sides in remaining butter.
Arrange 6 rings on prepared crust. In a bowl, beat eggs, sugar,
ricotta, cream cheese and vanilla until smooth; blend in
whipping cream. Pour cheese mixture into pan over apple
rings. Arrange remaining 6 rings on top and press apples
slightly under the mixture. Sprinkle top generously with
cinnamon. Bake at 450 degrees for 10 minutes, then reduce
heat to 300 degrees and bake for 50 to 55 minutes. Cool and
refrigerate overnight. Serves 6 to 8.

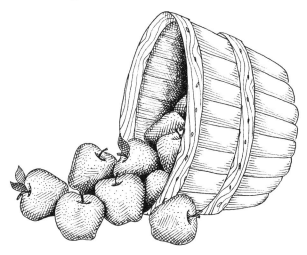

Sweet Pumpkin Bread

3 c. sugar
4 eggs, beaten
15-oz. can pumpkin
3-1/2 c. all-purpose flour
2 t. salt
1/2 t. cinnamon
1 t. baking powder

2 t. baking soda
1 t. nutmeg
1 c. oil
2/3 c. water
3 t. vanilla extract
1 c. chopped pecans

Beat sugar and eggs until fluffy; add pumpkin and mix well. In
a separate bowl, combine flour, salt, cinnamon, baking powder,
baking soda and nutmeg. Stir dry ingredients into pumpkin
mixture alternating with oil and water; add vanilla, mixing
well. Beat for 3 minutes; fold in nuts. Divide and pour into
3 greased 5"x3" loaf pans. Bake at 350 degrees for one hour;
brush hot glaze over tops of warm loaves. Makes 3 loaves.

Glaze:

1/2 c. sugar
1/4 c. water

1 t. vanilla extract

Mix ingredients together in a saucepan and boil for 3 minutes.

Sing a song of seasons!
Something bright in all!
Flowers in the Summer,
Fires in the Fall.
-Robert Louis Stevenson

Caramel Brownies

14-oz. pkg. caramels,
  unwrapped
2/3 c. evaporated milk,
  divided
18-1/4 oz. box German
  chocolate cake mix

2/3 c. butter
1 c. chopped pecans
12-oz. pkg. chocolate chips

Combine caramels and 1/3 cup milk in a microwave-safe bowl. Heat on low, stirring occasionally, until caramels have melted; set aside. In a separate bowl, combine cake mix with remaining milk and butter. Press half of cake mixture into a greased and floured 13"x9" baking pan; bake at 350 degrees for 8 minutes. Remove from oven. Scatter chocolate chips on crust, then drizzle melted caramel over chips. Drop remaining cake mixture by spoonfuls on top of caramels and continue to bake an additional 18 minutes. Cool before cutting into squares. Makes 10 to 12 servings.

Add a bundle of dried herbs to the fireplace...enjoy the fragrance while everyone settles in for dessert.

★ Classics ★

Old-Fashioned Spicy Pumpkin Pie

4 eggs, beaten
2 c. brown sugar
1/4 t. nutmeg
1 t. ground ginger
3 t. cinnamon
1/2 t. mace
1/2 t. cloves

1 t. salt
2 T. molasses
3 c. canned pumpkin
2 c. evaporated milk
2 9-inch pie crusts,
 prebaked

Thoroughly blend eggs, brown sugar, spices, salt, molasses
and pumpkin; add milk. Mix well and pour into crusts. Bake at
450 degrees for 10 minutes; reduce heat to 350 degrees and
continue baking for 30 minutes or until centers of pies are set.
Serves 12 to 15.

Cinnamon Hot Chocolate

1/4 c. baking cocoa
1/4 c. sugar
1 c. boiling water

3 c. milk
6-inch cinnamon stick
1 t. vanilla extract

Using a double boiler, combine cocoa and sugar; slowly add
water. Bring to a boil for 2 minutes. Add milk and cinnamon
stick; heat for 10 minutes. Remove cinnamon stick and add
vanilla; stir quickly to froth milk. Serves 4.

Make "real" whipped cream for pies...it's so much better
than store-bought! Just whip heavy cream until fluffy,
and then blend in sugar and vanilla extract to taste.

Chocolate Chip-Oatmeal Cookies

1/2 c. butter, softened
3/4 c. brown sugar, packed
1 egg
1 t. vanilla extract
1 c. all-purpose flour
1/2 t. baking soda

1/2 t. salt
1 c. semi-sweet chocolate
  chips
1 c. quick-cooking oats,
  uncooked
3/4 c. chopped walnuts

Cream together butter and sugar; blend in egg and vanilla and set aside. In a separate bowl, combine flour, baking soda and salt. Slowly add flour mixture to butter mixture, blending well. Fold in chocolate chips, oats and walnuts. Refrigerate dough at least 3 hours or overnight. Shape dough into one-inch balls and place on greased and floured baking sheets. Bake at 375 degrees for 12 to 15 minutes. Makes 2 dozen.

Cookies make a terrific gift for dinner guests to take home. Wrapped up in cello bags tied with raffia they're a tasty reminder of a day spent together.

Day-After Turkey Muffin Cups

1/4 c. celery, finely chopped	2 T. mayonnaise
3 T. green pepper, chopped	1/2 t. salt
1/4 c. onion, chopped	1/2 c. chopped almonds
1 T. margarine	12-oz. tube refrigerated
2 c. turkey, cooked and	biscuits
cubed	

Sauté celery, pepper and onion in margarine in a skillet until
tender. Add turkey, mayonnaise, salt and almonds; mix
thoroughly. Evenly press each biscuit in a greased muffin cup.
Spoon turkey mixture evenly into biscuit cups. Bake at
350 degrees for 15 to 20 minutes or until biscuits are golden.
Makes 10 cups.

Relax the day after Thanksgiving! Leftovers make it
easy...turkey sandwiches, casseroles and
soups make mealtime a snap.

Ham 'n Turkey Casserole

3 stalks celery, chopped
1/4 c. butter
1/4 c. all-purpose flour
1/2 t. salt
1 c. chicken broth
1 c. light cream
2 T. orange or pineapple
    juice
3-oz. can mushrooms

2 t. dried, minced onion
2 t. mustard
1 c. sour cream
2 c. cooked noodles
1-1/2 c. turkey, cooked
    and cubed
1-1/2 c. cooked ham, cubed
1/4 c. slivered almonds,
    toasted

Sauté celery in butter until tender; stir in flour and salt. Add broth and cream; cook until thick and bubbling, stirring constantly. Stir in juice, then add all remaining ingredients except almonds. Pour mixture in an ungreased 2-quart baking dish; top with almonds. Bake at 325 degrees for 25 to 35 minutes. Serves 6.

Slow cookers are ideal for hearty soups and stews.
Find a favorite recipe, toss the ingredients in
and forget about it until dinner time!

Turkey-Rice Casserole

10-3/4 oz. can cream of
   mushroom soup
10-3/4 oz. can cream of
   celery soup
1-1/2 c. milk

1-1/2 oz. pkg. dry onion
   soup mix
3 c. prepared rice
2 to 3 c. turkey, cooked
   and cubed

Combine all ingredients in an ungreased 2-quart baking dish.
Bake, covered, at 350 degrees for 35 minutes; uncover and
bake an additional 10 minutes. Makes 4 to 6 servings.

Turkey Pot Pie

4 c. chicken broth
3 carrots, peeled and cubed
2 potatoes, peeled and cubed
1 onion, chopped
1/3 c. all-purpose flour
1/4 c. plus 1 t. cold water,
   divided
salt and pepper to taste

1/2 t. nutmeg
10-oz. pkg. frozen peas
3 c. turkey, cooked
   and cubed
4 9-inch refrigerated pie
   crusts
1 egg

Heat broth, carrots, potatoes and onion in a saucepan until
boiling; reduce heat and simmer 15 to 20 minutes until
potatoes are tender. In a mixing bowl, stir flour into 1/4 cup
cold water to make a paste; whisk into hot broth. Add salt,
pepper and nutmeg; simmer 15 to 20 minutes until thickened.
Stir in peas and turkey; heat through. Unfold 2 pie crusts and
let sit 15 minutes. Place one in each of 2 pie pans and bake at
425 degrees for 8 to 10 minutes. Pour turkey mixture into
baked crusts and top with remaining crusts; vent tops. Blend
together egg and remaining water; brush over crusts. Bake at
425 degrees for 15 to 20 minutes. Serves 16.

Hearty Turkey Soup

2 T. oil
2 c. mushrooms, sliced
8 c. chicken broth
1/3 c. pearled barley,
   uncooked
1/4 c. dried, minced onion
1 t. dried sage

1/8 t. pepper
1-1/2 c. carrot, sliced
1-1/2 c. celery, sliced
1-1/2 c. zucchini, sliced
1 c. tomato, diced
2 c. turkey, cooked and
   chopped

Heat oil in a large saucepan; add mushrooms and sauté about 5 minutes or until tender. Stir in chicken broth, barley, onion, sage and pepper. Bring mixture to a boil, reduce heat and simmer, covered, for 20 minutes or until barley is almost tender. Stir in carrot, celery, zucchini and tomato; cover and simmer for 10 minutes. Add turkey and continue to cook, covered, about 15 minutes or until barley and vegetables are tender. Serves 4 to 6.

Invite neighbors over for a Soup Supper. Everyone brings a favorite soup to share and it's a great way to unwind and and enjoy the crisp, Autumn weather!

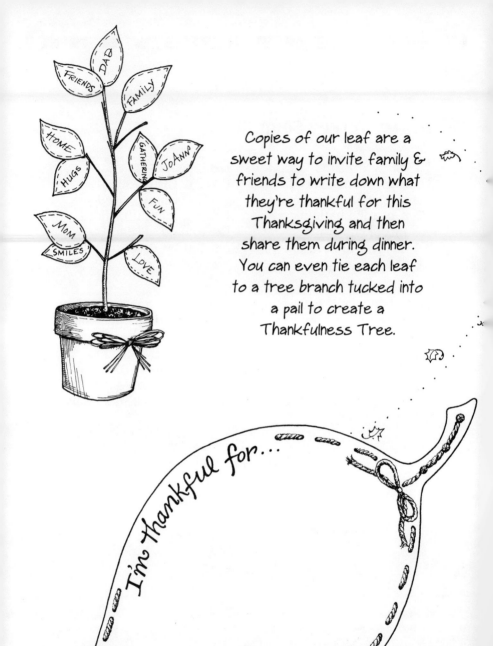

Copies of our leaf are a sweet way to invite family & friends to write down what they're thankful for this Thanksgiving and then share them during dinner. You can even tie each leaf to a tree branch tucked into a pail to create a Thankfulness Tree.

I'm thankful for...

Photocopy, cut out and write names on our Autumn placecard. If you'd like, add color with colored pencils and just fold in half...so simple!

Vickie

Index

Apple Cider Turkey..11
Baked Creamed Corn...6
Banana & Walnut Bread.....................................19
Caramel Brownies...23
Cheddar Biscuits with Garlic Butter.....................16
Cheesy Cauliflower..6
Chocolate Chip-Oatmeal Cookies.......................25
Cinnamon Hot Chocolate...................................24
Cinnamon Rolls..3
Country Glazed Ham...17
Cranberry Relish...13
Creamy Butternut Soup......................................18
Day-After Turkey Muffin Cups............................26
Garlic Mashed Potatoes......................................9
Glazed Spiced Pecans...5
Green Beans Supreme..15
Ham 'n Turkey Casserole....................................27
Harvest Apple Cheesecake.................................21
Hearty Turkey Soup...29
Heavenly Potatoes...16
Herbed Rice Pilaf..11
Homestyle Stuffing..14
Make-Ahead Dinner Rolls..................................12
Maple Indian Pudding.......................................20
Old-Fashioned Spicy Pumpkin Pie......................24
Orange-Apple Cider..4
Perfectly Pecan Pie...20
Pumpkin Coffeecake...2
Pumpkin Dip...5
Pumpkin Farmer's Casserole..............................18
Roast Turkey & Gravy..10
Spiced Apple Tea...4
Sweet Pumpkin Bread.......................................22
Triple Cranberry Sauce......................................13
Turkey Pot Pie..28
Turkey-Rice Casserole 28
Vanilla-Glazed Sweet Potatoes 8
Yam & Apple Bake 7